This book given
by
Alice Fabro Edwards
in memory of her husband
Bill Edwards
2002

The United States

Vermont

Paul Joseph
ABDO & Daughters

visit us at
www.abdopub.com

Published by Abdo & Daughters, 4940 Viking Drive, Suite 622, Edina, Minnesota 55435.
Copyright © 1998 by Abdo Consulting Group, Inc., Pentagon Tower, P.O. Box 36036,
Minneapolis, Minnesota 55435 USA. International copyrights reserved in all countries.
No part of this book may be reproduced in any form without written permission from the
publisher.

Printed in the United States.

Cover and Interior Photo credits: Peter Arnold, Inc., Archive, Corbis-Bettmann

Edited by Lori Kinstad Pupeza
Contributing editor Brooke Henderson
Special thanks to our Checkerboard Kids—Teddy Borth, Shane Wagner, Aisha Baker

All statistics taken from the 1990 census; The Rand McNally Discovery Atlas of The
United States.

Library of Congress Cataloging-in-Publication Data

Joseph, Paul, 1970-
    Vermont / Paul Joseph.
    p.   cm. -- (United States)
    Includes index.
    Summary: Surveys the history, geography, and people of the state that is
    nicknamed the "Green Mountain State."
    ISBN 1-56239-886-5
    1. Vermont--Juvenile literature. [1. Vermont.] I. Title. II. series: United
    States (Series)
    F49.3.J67   1998
    974.3--dc21
                                                            97-27136
                                                            CIP
                                                            AC

Contents

Welcome to Vermont

Vermont is one of the smallest states in the country. With just over 500,000 people, only two states have a smaller **population**. In land size, only seven states are smaller than Vermont.

Even though the state is very small, it has a lot of history, tradition, people, and beauty. Vermont has many things to do for both the people living there and the many visitors. Mountains, lakes, forests, and rivers make the state one of the most scenic in the land.

The early name of the region was New Hampshire Grants. In 1777, it was renamed New Connecticut. It was later changed to its present name, Vermont.

The name Vermont came from two French words that mean "green" and "mountain." Vermont is known for its beautiful green mountains. In fact it is nicknamed the "Green Mountain State."

Vermont lies in the northeast part of the United States. This area is also called New England.

Vermont is called the Green Mountain State.

Fun Facts

VERMONT
Capital
Montpelier (8,247 people)
Area
9,273 square miles
(24,017 sq km)
Population
564,964 people
Rank: 48th
Statehood
March 4, 1791
(14th state admitted)
Principal river
Connecticut River
Highest point
Mount Mansfield;
4,393 feet (1,339 m)
Largest city
Burlington (39,127 people)
Motto
Freedom and unity
Song
"Hail, Vermont"
Famous People
Ethan Allen, Chester Arthur,
Calvin Coolidge, George Dewey,
Stephen Douglas

*S*tate Flag

*R*ed Clover

*H*ermit Thrush

*S*ugar Maple

About Vermont

The Green Mountain State

Detail area

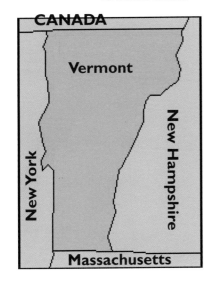

VT

Vermont's
abbreviation

Borders: west (New York), north (Canada), east (New Hampshire), south (Massachusetts)

Nature's Treasures

The beautiful state of Vermont has many treasures. The scenic Green Mountains provide **tourists** with excellent views. In the Green Mountains is Mount Mansfield, the highest point in the state at 4,393 feet (1,339 m). People love to ski down Vermont's many mountain ranges.

In the summer months Lake Champlain and other clear mountain lakes attract thousands of tourists for boating, fishing, and other water sports.

There are over four million acres of forest in the state. Two of the most valuable trees are the white pine and sugar maple. The wood from pine trees is made into furniture. The sap in the maple trees is made into maple syrup. Every fall, lots of apples grow on Vermont's trees. People all over America eat apples from trees in Vermont.

Underground the state has many treasures too. These treasures are called **minerals**. Stone is the most valuable mineral. Marble, which is found in western Vermont, has been used in many buildings, including the United States Supreme Court building.

Windsurfing on Lake Champlain, Vermont.

Beginnings

In 1609, Samuel de Champlain and his group entered Vermont. They paddled up a lake on the western part of the state that was later named after him, Lake Champlain. For more than 100 years, however, the area was never settled.

The English made the first settlement at Fort Dummer in 1724. Beginning in 1749, the governor of New Hampshire gave out **grants** of land for new towns in the Vermont region. This is why the area was first known as New Hampshire Grants.

These people from New Hampshire began settling in Vermont. These **settlers** cleared forests, built cabins to live in, and planted **crops** so they could eat and survive.

In 1775, America declared its independence from England. This started a war called the **American**

Revolution. The American Revolution was fought between America and England.

One of the first important victories in the American Revolution was led by a group of people from Vermont. The group was known as the Green Mountain Boys. They were led by Ethan Allen.

Vermont declared itself a state in 1777. The other states around it had to agree with the **borders** that Vermont set. Years later, Massachusetts, New Hampshire, and New York finally agreed to the borders. On March 4, 1791, Vermont became the 14th state.

Ethan Allen and the capture of Fort Ticonderoga.

B.C. to 1724

Early People and Land

During the Ice Age, many thousands of years ago, Vermont was covered by ice and glaciers. Later, the ice began to melt and the land of Vermont began to form.

1609: Samuel de Champlain and his group of French **explorers** enter Vermont.

1724: People from Massachusetts build Fort Dummer. It is the first time people settle in Vermont and plan to stay there.

Vermont

B.C. to 1724

1763 to 1834

Statehood and Beyond

 1763: France gives Vermont to England.

 1775: America begins to fight against England for its independence.

 1791: Vermont becomes the 14th state on March 4.

 1834: Thomas Davenport invents the world's first electric motor at Brandon, Vermont.

Vermont

1763 to 1834

1881 to 1961

Presidents to Today

1881: Chester Arthur of Fairfield, Vermont, becomes the 21st president of the United States.

1923: Calvin Coolidge of Plymouth, Vermont, becomes the 30th president of the United States.

1927: Terrible floods ruin a large part of Vermont.

1961: Ball Mountain Dam on the West River is completed. It is the highest dam in the state at 275 feet (84 m).

Vermont

1881 to 1961

Montpelier

Vermont's People

There are just over a half million people in the state of Vermont. It is the second smallest state in the country.

Many well-known people have come from Vermont. Among them are two presidents of the United States— Chester A. Arthur and Calvin Coolidge. Arthur, who was born in Fairfield, Vermont, became the 21st president in 1881.

Coolidge, who was born in Plymouth, Vermont, became the 30th president in 1923. Both men were vice presidents of the United States before becoming presidents.

Some very famous inventors were from Vermont. John Deere of Rutland, Vermont, made the first steel plowshare. Today, the John Deere Company sells farm machinery all over the world. They sell many different kinds of tractors and plows.

Thomas Davenport was born in Williamstown, Vermont. He invented the first electric motor in 1834. He invented many other motor-driven machines, including the first electric car.

Calvin Coolidge

John Deere

Splendid Cities

Vermont doesn't have any large cities. In fact, the biggest city has less than 40,000 people. But these small cities and towns are still splendid and offer many things to do and see.

About two out of every three people that live in Vermont live in **rural** areas. The rest of the people in the state live in towns and cities. Only three cites in the state have more than 15,000 people living in them.

Burlington is the largest city in the state with just under 40,000 people. It is known for its **manufacturing industry**. The town is home to Ethan Allen's gravesite. Many people visit this grave each year. The

University of Vermont and Trinity College are also in Vermont.

Montpelier is the capital of Vermont. The city sits almost in the center of the state. Nearby are many ski **resort** towns like Stowe. Colchester is a farming community on Lake Champlain. Many people visit this area in the summer for the wonderful weather and the beautiful lake.

Autumn at Island Pond, Vermont.

Vermont's Land

During the Ice Age, Vermont was covered by huge glaciers. After these great ice sheets began to melt, the land of Vermont began to form. The state is divided into five distinct regions.

The Champlain Valley region covers the western part of the state, around Lake Champlain. The lake is the lowest point in the state.

The Taconic Mountains region is in the southwest part of the state. This region has many mountain ranges, valleys, and lakes.

The Green Mountains region is the largest region in the state. It stretches from the very top of the state to the very bottom.

White Mts. Region

Champlain Valley

Green Mountains

New England Upland

Taconic Mts.

22

This area is filled with forests and mountains. It is an excellent place to visit for **tourists**. Also in this region is Mount Mansfield, the highest point in the state.

The New England Upland region also reaches from top to the bottom of the state. It is just east of the Green Mountains. This area has many streams, lakes, and rivers. It also has deep valleys and high mountain ridges.

The White Mountain region is in the very northeast part of Vermont. This area has very few people because it is a mountainous wilderness.

A maple tree in the Green Mountains of Vermont.

Vermont at Play

The people of Vermont and the many people who visit the state have a lot of things to do.

Every summer thousands of **tourists** visit Lake Champlain for boating, fishing, swimming, water skiing, and other water sports. Lake Memphremagog is another excellent lake in Vermont. This lake also stretches into Canada for 37 miles (60 km).

Many visitors enjoy the wonderful hiking trails of Vermont. The most popular hiking route is Long Trail. It follows along the Green Mountains for more than 260 miles (418 kilometers). Besides the excellent trails, the views are some of the best in the country.

In the fall, people come to Vermont to see the leaves change color.

In the winter, many tourists come to Vermont for skiing. There are more than 15 major downhill ski **resorts**. Some of the best resorts in the state include those at Killington, Stowe, Stratton Mountain, and West Dover.

Vermont also has many museums and historic sites. Among them is the Bennington Battle Monument and the Old Constitution House. The Shelburne Museum, near Burlington, is a 45-acre area that shows what life was like when the first **settlers** lived in Vermont. It has old barns, shops, and houses.

Hiking and climbing are popular pastimes in Vermont.

Vermont at Work

The people of Vermont must work to make money. Because there are not a lot of large cities in the state, most people work in **rural** communities and on farms.

Vermont has many visitors each year making service a large business in the state. Service is working in restaurants, hotels, and **resorts**.

However, more people in the state of Vermont work in **manufacturing** than any other job in the state. The biggest manufacturing **industry** in the state is the making of electrical and electronic parts.

Vermont has about 7,000 farms in the state and most are dairy farms. People work in dairy farms making milk and cheese.

Other farmers in the state grow corn, potatoes, and oats. The most valuable **crop** is apples. Most farmers grow their apples along the shores of Lake Champlain.

Vermont offers many different things to do and see. Because of its natural beauty, people, land, lakes, and **resorts**, the Green Mountain State is a great place to visit, live, work, and play.

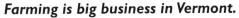
Farming is big business in Vermont.

Fun Facts

• When Samuel de Champlain first came to Vermont he mapped out the area. The French **explorer** named the thick evergreen mountains Verd Mont on his map. In French, those words mean "green mountain." That is how the state got its name Vermont.

• Montpelier has been Vermont's capital since 1805. Before that time the capital was in various cities including Windsor and Rutland.

• The highest point in Vermont is Mount Mansfield. It is 4,393 feet (1,339 m) tall. The lowest level in the state is Lake Champlain. It is only 95 feet (29 m).

• Vermont's land size is not very big. Its area is 9,273 square miles (24,017 sq km). In land size only seven other states are smaller. In **population** only two other states have less people.

•Vermont's longest length from north to south is 159 miles (256 km). Its longest width from east to west is 89 miles (143 km). Its shortest width is only 37 miles (60 km) in the southern part of the state.

The White Mountains are part of the beautiful scenery in Vermont.

Glossary

American Revolution: a war that gave the United States its independence from Great Britain.

Border: neighboring states, countries, or waters.

Crops: what farmers grow on their farm to either eat or sell or do both.

Explorers: people that are one of the first to discover and look over land.

Grant: a paper that gave land to a person from the government.

Industry: many different types of businesses.

Manufacture: to make things by machine in a factory.

Minerals: things found in the earth, such as gold, diamonds, or coal.

Population: the number of people living in a certain place.

Resort: a place to vacation that has fun things to do.

Rural: outside of the city.

Settlers: people that move to a new land and build a community.

Tourists: people who travel for fun.

Internet Sites

Discover Vermont
http://discover-vermont.com/
Welcome to Discover Vermont, the online guide to the Green Mountain State.

Vermont, The Green Mountain State
http://mole.uvm.edu/Vermont/
History, government, treasures, recreational areas, and much more.

These sites are subject to change. Go to your favorite search engine and type in Vermont for more sites.

PASS IT ON

Tell Others Something Special About Your State

To educate readers around the country, pass on interesting tips, places to see, history, and little unknown facts about the state you live in. We want to hear from you!

To get posted on ABDO & Daughters website, e-mail us at "mystate@abdopub.com"

Index